Joseph

Oregon

C-
979.5
Jx

DATE DUE

1998

PRINTED IN U.S.A.

The United States

Oregon

Paul Joseph
ABDO & Daughters

visit us at
www.abdopub.com

Published by Abdo & Daughters, 4940 Viking Drive, Suite 622, Edina, Minnesota 55435.
Copyright © 1998 by Abdo Consulting Group, Inc., Pentagon Tower, P.O. Box 36036,
Minneapolis, Minnesota 55435 USA. International copyrights reserved in all countries.
No part of this book may be reproduced in any form without written permission from the
publisher.

Printed in the United States.

Cover and Interior Photo credits: Peter Arnold, Inc., SuperStock, Archive, Corbis-
Bettmann

Edited by Lori Kinstad Pupeza
Contributing editor Brooke Henderson
Special thanks to our Checkerboard Kids—Priscilla Cáceres, Raymond Sherman,
Kenny Abdo

All statistics taken from the 1990 census; The Rand McNally Discovery Atlas of The
United States.

Library of Congress Cataloging-in-Publication Data

Joseph, Paul, 1970-
    Oregon / by Paul Joseph.
    p.   cm. -- (United States)
    Includes index.
    Summary: Surveys the people, geography, and history of the northwestern
    Beaver State.
    ISBN 1-56239-878-4
    1. Oregon--Juvenile literature. [1. Oregon.] I. Title. II. Series: United States
    (series).
    F876.3.J67   1998
    979.5--dc21
                                                        97-21421
                                                        CIP
                                                        AC

Contents

Welcome to Oregon

The name Oregon comes from the French word *ouragan*, which means "hurricane." The French called the Columbia River a hurricane. However, when the English were going to explore the area in the 1700s, they called it "Ouragon" and "Ourigan." In 1778, the current spelling was used in a travel book.

Oregon was nicknamed the Beaver State because there were so many beaver **pelts** in the state. Fur traders used the beaver pelts as money. Today, the fur trade has been replaced by other trades in the state.

Oregon cuts more lumber than any other state. This, plus farms, **mines**, **fisheries**, and **manufacturing** make Oregon a very important state. The Beaver State lies in northwestern United States.

Many people visit this beautiful state each year. There are so many wonderful things to do there. Oregon is filled with scenic mountains, incredible forests, state parks, lakes, rivers, and sandy beaches of the Pacific Ocean.

Smith Rocks State Park near Redmond, Oregon.

Fun Facts

OREGON

Capital
Salem (107,786 people)
Area
96,187 square miles
(249,123 sq km)
Population
2,853,733 people
Rank: 29th
Statehood
February 14, 1859
(33rd state admitted)
Principal river
Columbia River
Highest point
Mount Hood;
11,235 feet (3,424 m)
Largest city
Portland (437,319 people)
Motto
The Union
Song
"Oregon, My Oregon"
Famous People
Robert Gray, Chief Joseph, Linus
Pauling

*S*tate Flag

*O*regon Grape

*W*estern
Meadowlark

*D*ouglas Fir

About Oregon

The Beaver State

Detail area

OR

Oregon's abbreviation

Borders: west (Pacific Ocean), north (Washington), east (Idaho), south (California, Nevada)

Nature's Treasures

Oregon has many wonderful treasures in its state. There are beautiful mountains, many lakes and rivers, the Pacific Ocean on its coast, and state forests.

Oregon's biggest treasure is its trees. The state has about 30 million acres of forests! The most common trees in the Beaver State are the Douglas fir and ponderosa pine.

Oregon's excellent weather and **fertile** soil help grow many rich crops. The state has about 37,000 farms. Oregon's land grows fruits and vegetables. There are also lots of flower farmers in Oregon. Eastern Oregon has a lot of land that animals use for **grazing**.

The temperature in the eastern part of Oregon is a perfect mix. In the summers it is very pleasant and cool. In the winters it remains nice, staying very mild. The west has more rain and snow. Here it is much hotter in the summer and colder in the winter.

Other important treasures in Oregon are the **minerals** found in the state. Although there are not a lot of minerals, some that are **mined** are stone, sand, gravel, gold, and silver.

The Pacific Ocean, rivers, and lakes make for great fishing. The main fish caught are tuna, salmon, crabs, clams, and oysters.

Anybody that has gone to Oregon will tell you that the best treasure in the state is its natural beauty.

A field of tulips in Oregon.

Beginnings

The first known people to live in Oregon were **Native Americans**. The largest group was the Chinook who lived in the northwest part of the state.

Some believe that European **explorers** saw the land now called Oregon as early as the 1500s. However, it wasn't until 1775 that Oregon was claimed by a country. Bruno Heceta discovered the Columbia River.

In 1778, James Cook, from Great Britain, explored Oregon. In 1805, Lewis and Clark made their famous journey through Oregon.

Many people began coming to Oregon to get rich from fur trading. Different countries wanted to own Oregon because of all the fur. In 1818, people from the United States and England began living in the Oregon area together.

American **settlements** were popping up everywhere in Oregon during the 1830s and 1840s. Finally, in 1846, England gave up Oregon to the United States. In 1848, the United States government created the Oregon Territory.

On February 14, 1859, Oregon joined the Union and became the 33rd state.

Native Americans in the early days of Oregon.

B.C. to 1775

Early Land, People, and Explorers

During the Ice Age, many thousands of years ago, Oregon was covered by huge glaciers of ice. Many years later the ice began to melt and the land formed.

The first known group to live in the area were **Native Americans**. The largest group were the Chinook. Other Native Americans were the Nez Perce, the Umatillahs, the Paiute, the Modoc, and the Klamath.

1602: Sebastian Vizcaino and Martin de Aquilar see the coast of Oregon.

1775: Bruno Heceta discovers the Columbia River.

12

Oregon
B.C. to 1775

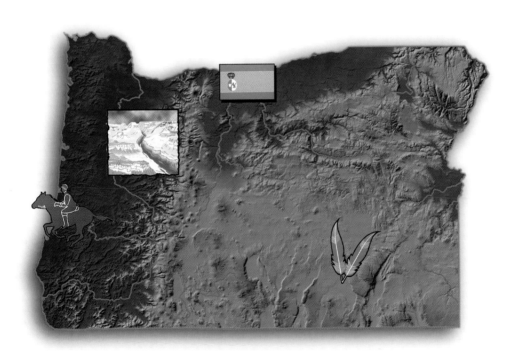

1800s

Ownership to Statehood

 1805: Lewis and Clark make their journey through Oregon.

 1818: The United States and England decide to live in Oregon together.

 1846: A treaty with England gives the United States all of Oregon.

 1848: The Oregon Territory is created. Oregon City becomes the capital. In 1850, Salem was made the capital.

 1859: Oregon becomes the 33rd state on February 14.

Oregon

1800s

The 1900s

Present Day Oregon

1902: Crater Lake National Park is created.

1955: A Freeway opens between Portland and Salem.

1977: The Portland Trail Blazers win their first and only NBA Championship behind the play of their star center Bill Walton.

1987: Devastating forest fires destroy around 300,000 acres of Oregon's land.

1990: Barbara Roberts is elected the first woman governor of Oregon.

Oregon

The 1900s

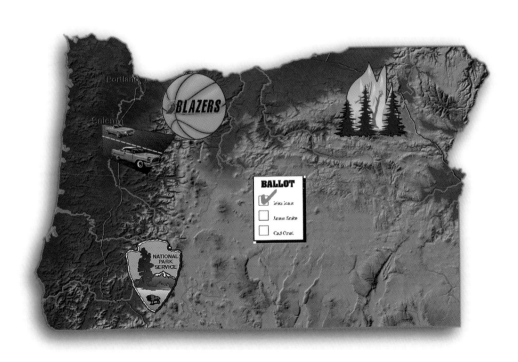

Oregon's People

There are just under three million people living in the state of Oregon. The first known people to live in Oregon were **Native Americans**. Today, there are about 38,500 Native Americans living in the state. Of these, almost 5,000 live on **reservations**.

A long time ago, many Chinese lived in eastern Oregon. This was their trading post. Today, Oregon ranks fourth in America for resettling refugees from Asia.

Many notable people have made Oregon home. Children's book author Beverly Cleary was born in McMinnville, Oregon. She's always had a strong following of young readers. Her books include Henry Huggins, Otis Spofford, Ramona the Pest, and Dear Mr. Henshaw.

Charles L. McNary was the **senator** of Oregon from 1917 to 1944. In 1940, he was the Republican candidate for vice president of the United States. Husband and wife, Richard and Maurine Neuberger, were both **senators** for Oregon. Maurine replaced her husband after he died in 1960, becoming only the third woman senator in United States history.

Barbara Roberts was the first woman governor of the state. And Doc Severinsen, born in Arlington, Oregon, is a great trumpet player and band leader.

Richard & Maurine Neuberger

Beverly Cleary

Doc Severinsen

Splendid Cities

Most of the large cities are located in the western part of the state. The biggest city by far is Portland. It has almost 500,000 people living in it. It has many different **industries** including lumber and wood products and the **manufacturing** of electrical things, like radios and light bulbs.

The city has many wonderful parks for fun outdoor activities. Portland State University is here. It is also home to the NBA's Portland Trail Blazers.

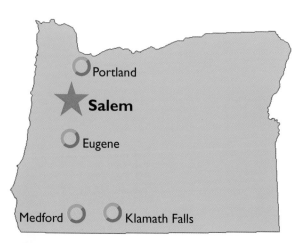

Eugene is the second largest city with just over 100,000 people. It is located on the Willamette River. It is known for its lumber mills and factories.

Salem is the capital and third largest city. It is located in a farming and dairy area.

A few other cities are Medford, Corvallis, Klamath Falls, Columbia, Springfield, Hillsboro, and Lake Oswego.

Portland, Oregon with Mt. Hood in the background.

Oregon's Land

Oregon has some of the most beautiful land in the country. About 100 to 150 miles (161 to 241 m) inland from the Pacific Ocean are the Cascade Mountains. These mountains divide the state into two sections.

One section is west of the mountains and covers about a third of the state. It is filled with deep valleys and heavy forests. This area gets a lot of rain. This area also has rivers and mountains. It also has the lowest point in the state and the highest. The highest point is Mount Hood, at 11,235 feet (3,424 m) tall. The lowest is at sea level.

The region west of the Cascade Mountains is divided into three areas.

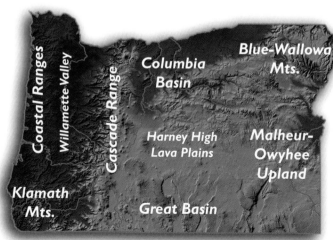

They are the Klamath Mountains, the Coastal Ranges, and the Willamette Valley.

The region east of the Cascade Mountains is much drier and the weather changes a lot. This area has many scenic lakes, rivers, mountains, and canyons.

This region is divided into five areas. They are the Columbia Basin, the Harney High Lava Plains, the Great Basin, the Blue-Wallowa Mountains, and the Malheur-Owyhee Upland.

The Pacific Ocean on the coast of Oregon.

Oregon at Play

The people of Oregon and the many people who visit the state have a lot of things to do. The outdoors offers the most fun in the state. There are mountains, rivers, lakes, the Pacific Ocean, canyons, forests, and parks.

During some of the months a person could be water-skiing and snow-skiing in the same day. In the ocean or lakes people can swim, boat, or fish. In the mountains people can ski, climb, or hike. At both places people can just sit and look at the natural beauty.

In the forests people can hike. There are many animals, trees, and wild flowers in these wonderful forests.

There are also many other activities that do not include the scenic sights of Oregon. The Oregon Shakespeare Festival in Ashland attracts thousands of viewers in the summer.

The Pendleton Round-Up recalls the days of the Old West. People also go to the World Championship Timber Carnival in Albany and the Rose Festival in Portland.

Oregon has some of the finest museums, libraries, and colleges. Oregon also has professional sports. The Portland Trail Blazers play in the National Basketball Association.

Children playing on one of Oregon's many beaches.

Oregon at Work

The people of Oregon must work to make money. Many people work in or around large cities, while others work in **rural** communities.

A lot of people work in **manufacturing**. Since forests cover nearly half of the state, lumber manufacturing provides many jobs.

Other manufacturing jobs are the making of food products, printing, publishing, and making electronic equipment.

Many people in the state of Oregon are farmers. There are about 18 million acres of land for the 37,000 farms in the state. There are a lot of dairy farms. Many farmers grow crops like flower bulbs, cranberries, plums, prunes, and sweet corn.

Some people in Oregon work in **fisheries**. Along with the Pacific Ocean, rivers and lakes also have many fish. Some of the best catches include albacore tuna, salmon, crabs, clams, and oysters.

There are many different things to do and see in the great state of Oregon. Because of its natural beauty, people, land, mountains, and forests, the Beaver State is a great place to visit, live, work, and play.

Loggers on Oregon's Mt. Hood.

Fun Facts

•In 1848, the Oregon Territory was created. Oregon City was named the capital. In 1850 the capital was moved to Salem. In 1859, Oregon became a state. Today, Salem is still the capital.

•The highest point in Oregon is Mount Hood. It is 11,235 feet (3,424 m) tall. The lowest point in the state is sea level.

•Every year in Portland, one of the largest children's parades goes on during the rose festival.

•From east to west Oregon stretches 395 miles (636 km). From north to south the state reaches 295 miles (475 km). The Pacific Ocean coastline of Oregon is 296 miles (476 km) long.

•Crater Lake in Oregon was formed by the collapse of the peak of Mount Mazama more than 7,700 years ago.

Melting snow from the mountains helps fill the nearly 2,000-feet (610-m) deep lake! It's the deepest in the United States.

Crater Lake in Oregon.

Glossary

Explorers: people that are one of the first to discover and look over land.

Fertile: able to make things grow well.

Fisheries: the business of catching fish.

Graze: animals eating grass.

Industry: many different types of businesses.

Manufacture: to make things by machine in a factory.

Minerals: things found in the earth, such as rock, diamonds, or coal.

Mining: working underground to get minerals.

Native Americans: the first people who were born in and occupied North America.

Pelt: the skin of a fury animal.

Population: the number of people living in a certain place.

Reservations: an area of land where Native Americans live, work, and have their own laws.

Rural: outside of the city.

Senator: one of two elected officials from a state that represents the state in Washington, D.C. There they make laws and are part of Congress.

Settlements: the places where people move to and build a new community. A new land where they haven't lived before.

Internet Sites

Edge of Oregon
http://www.europa.com/edge/oregon.html
This is a list of cool places and hot spots here in Oregon. If anyone has any points of interest to add, your input is appreciated. Hundreds of links that include attractions, adventures, mysteries, and many other Oregon hot spots.

Welcome to Oregon
http://www.el.com/To/Oregon/
Oregon is a dramatic land of many changes. From the rugged seacoast, the high mountain passes of the Oregon Cascades, the lush greenery and magnificent waterfalls of the Columbia Gorge, to the lava and Ponderosa pines of the high desert, Oregon's natural beauty has been preserved for all to experience and enjoy through the internet.

These sites are subject to change. Go to your favorite search engine and type in Oregon for more sites.

PASS IT ON

Tell Others Something Special About Your State

To educate readers around the country, pass on interesting tips, places to see, history, and little unknown facts about the state you live in. We want to hear from you!

To get posted on ABDO & Daughters website, e-mail us at "mystate@abdopub.com"

Index